Decorative Patterns

This coloring book belongs to the creative

Email **rania_mousa@hotmail.com**
to stay connected for exciting new releases

ISBN-13:   978-1986651998
ISBN-10:   1986651991

Try your colors here

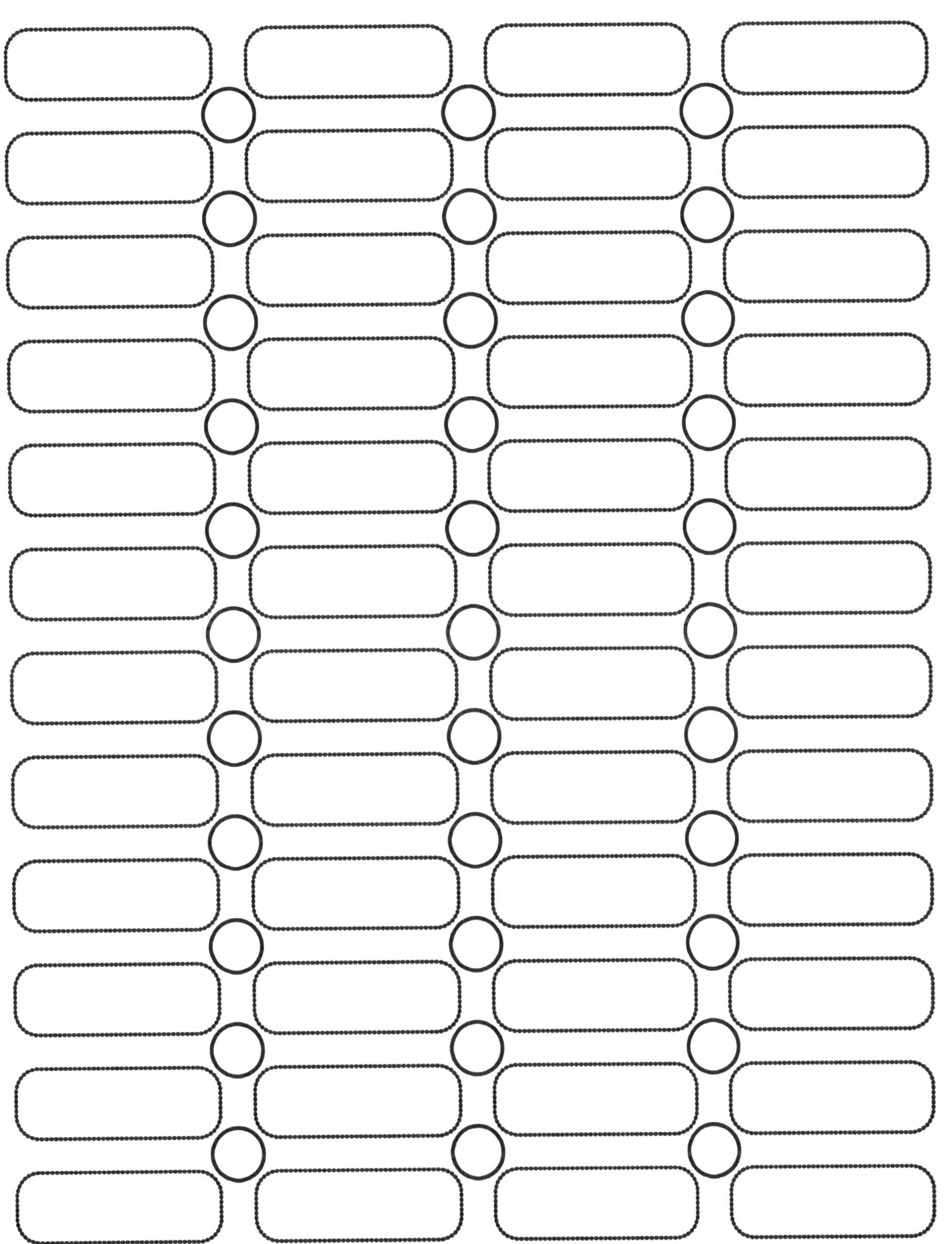

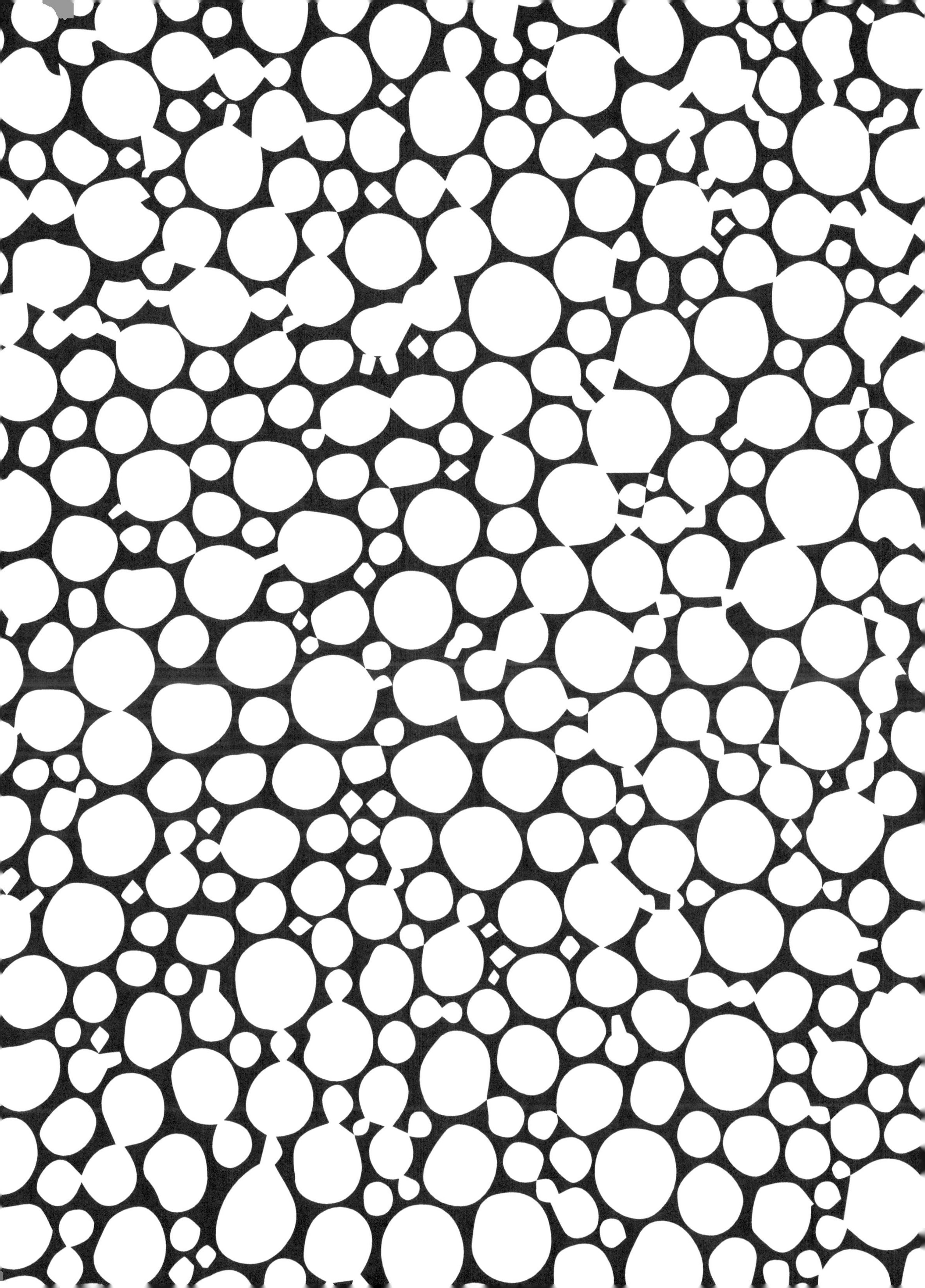

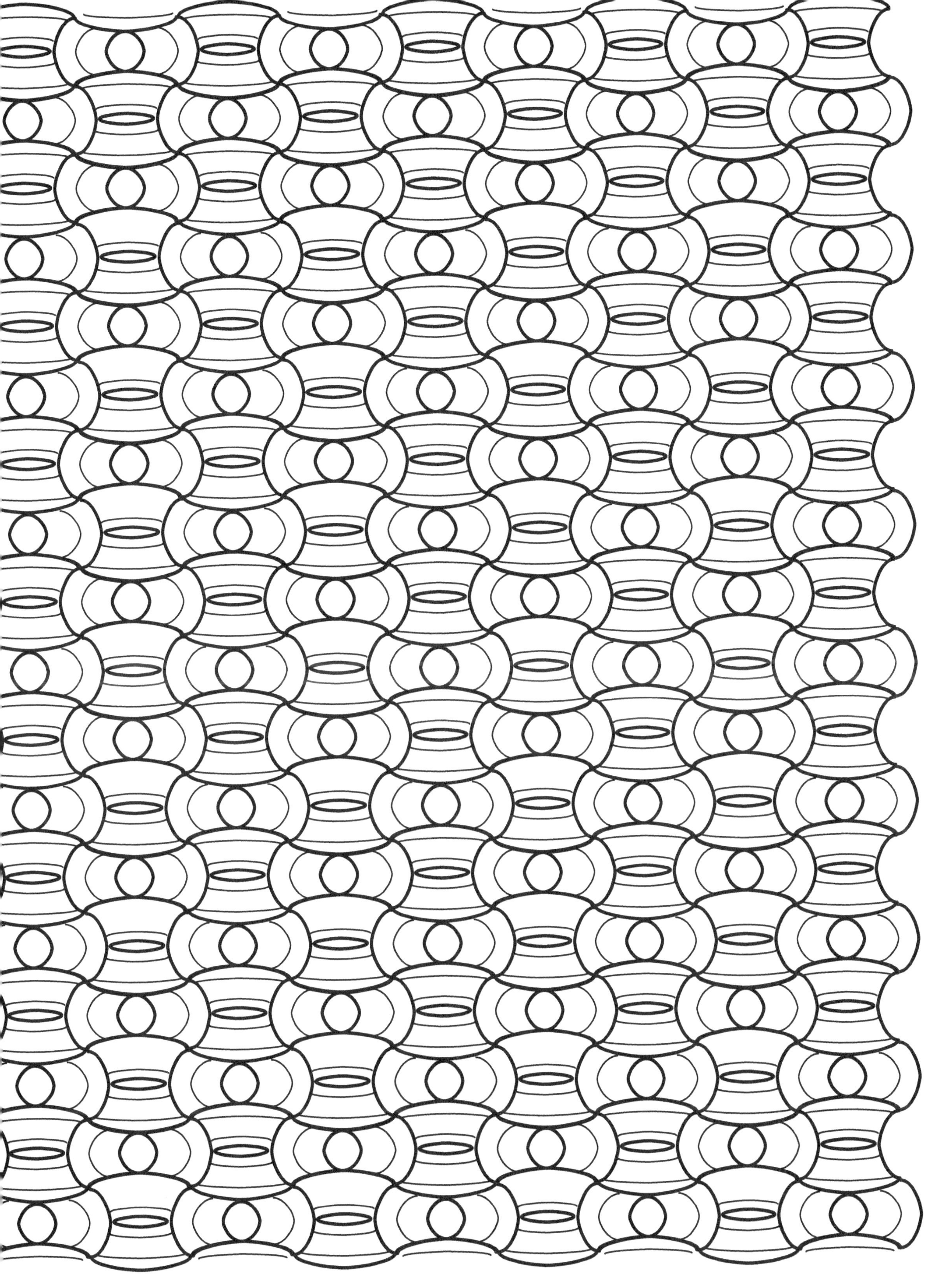

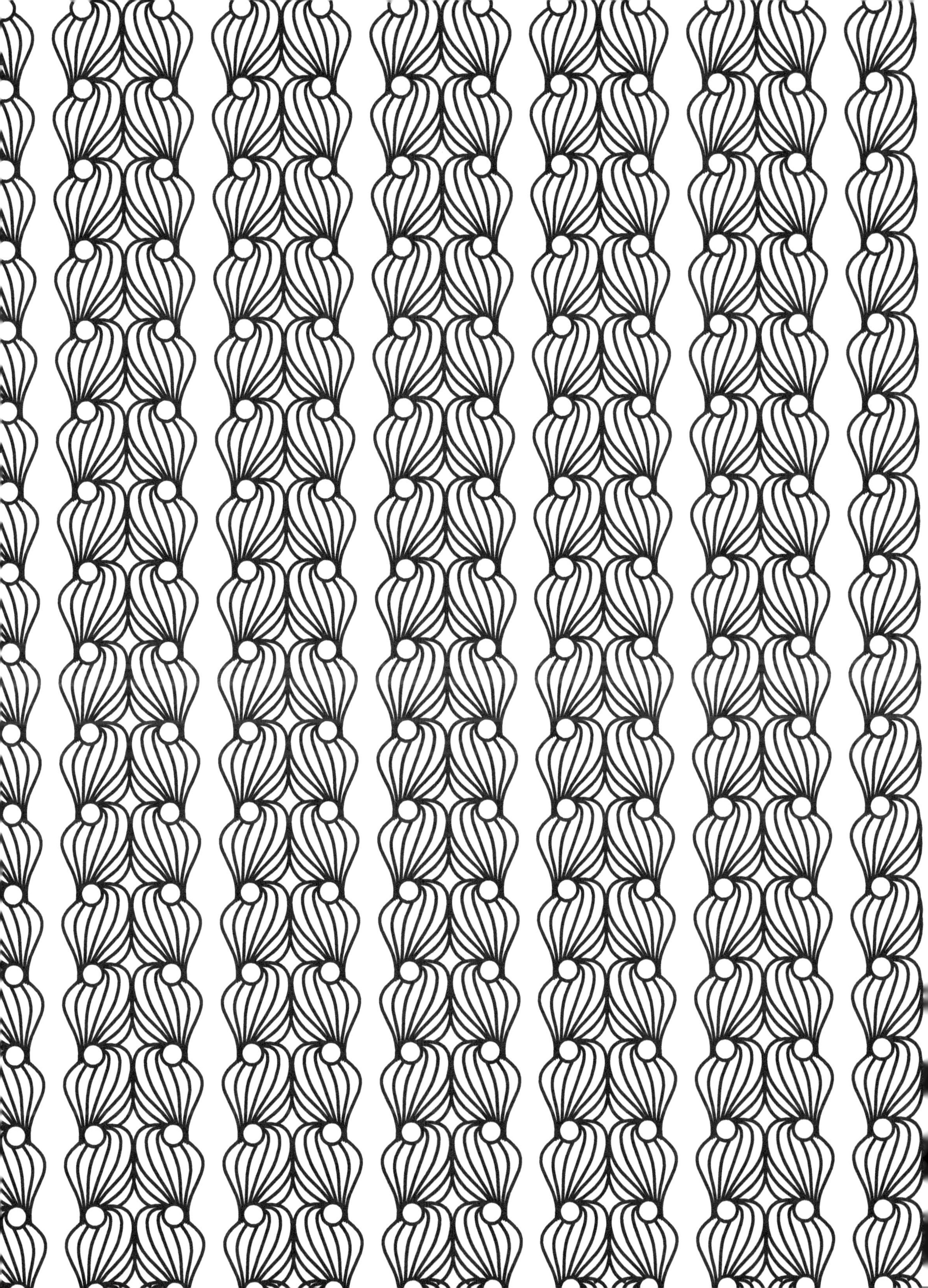

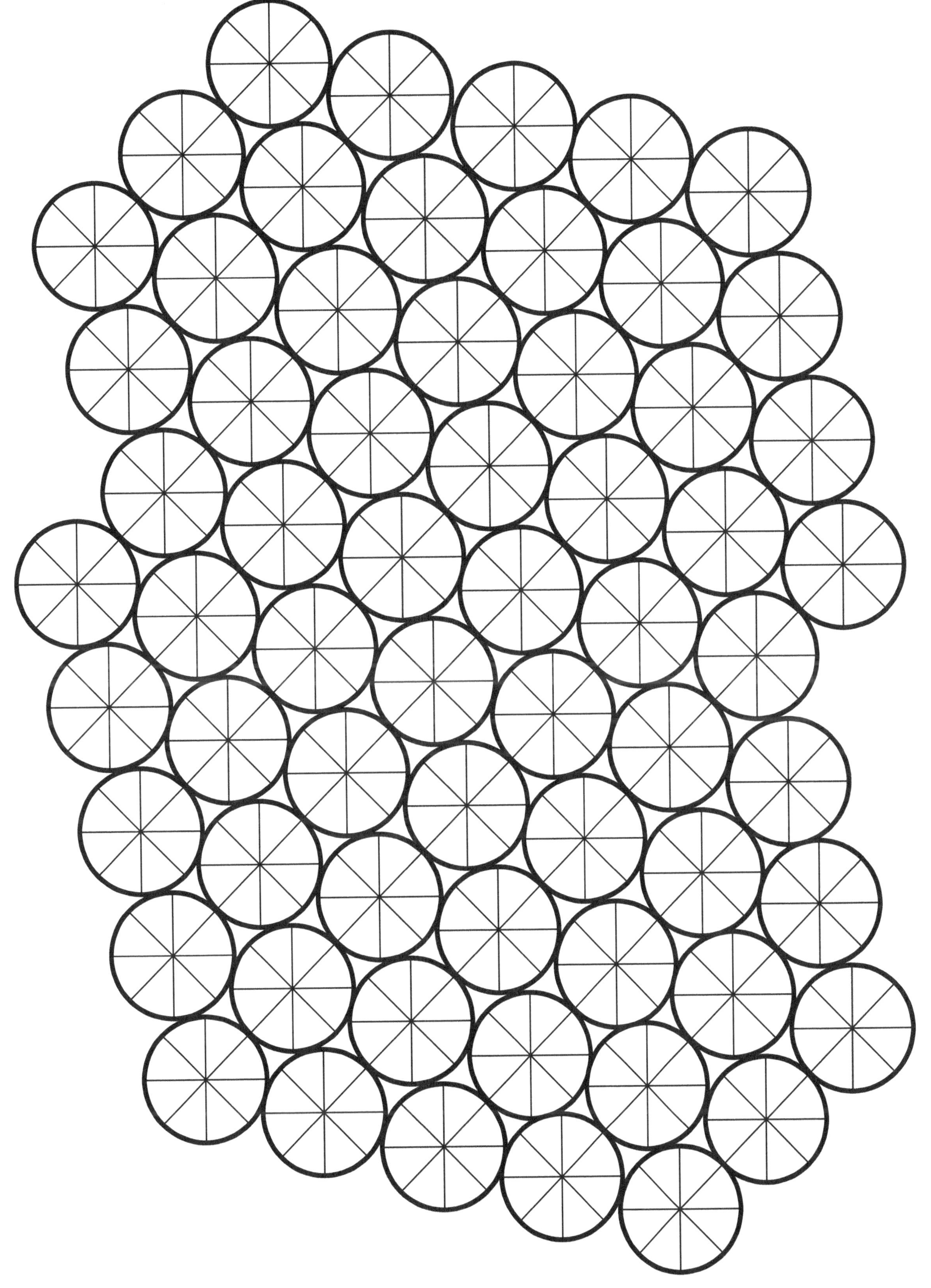

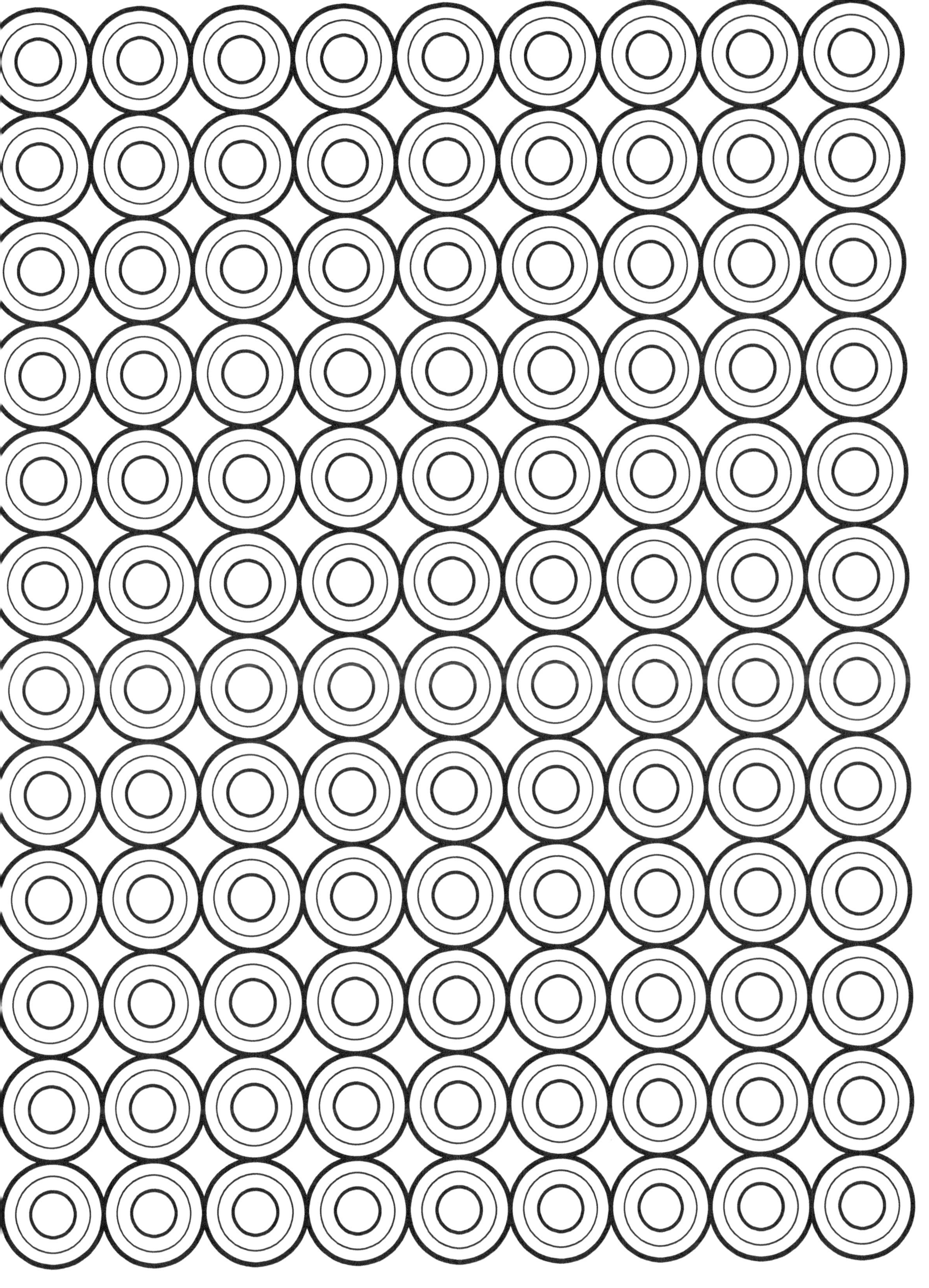

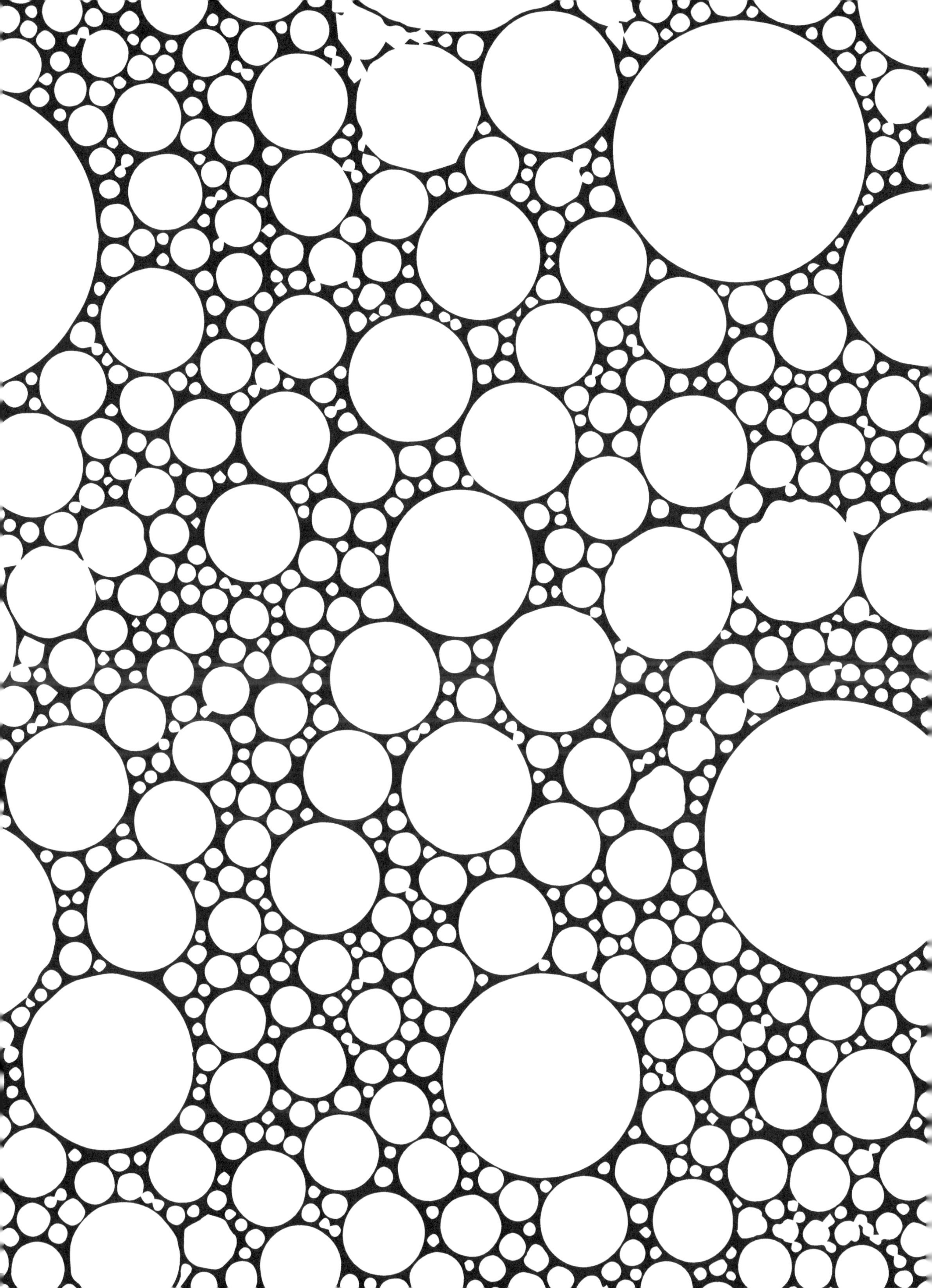

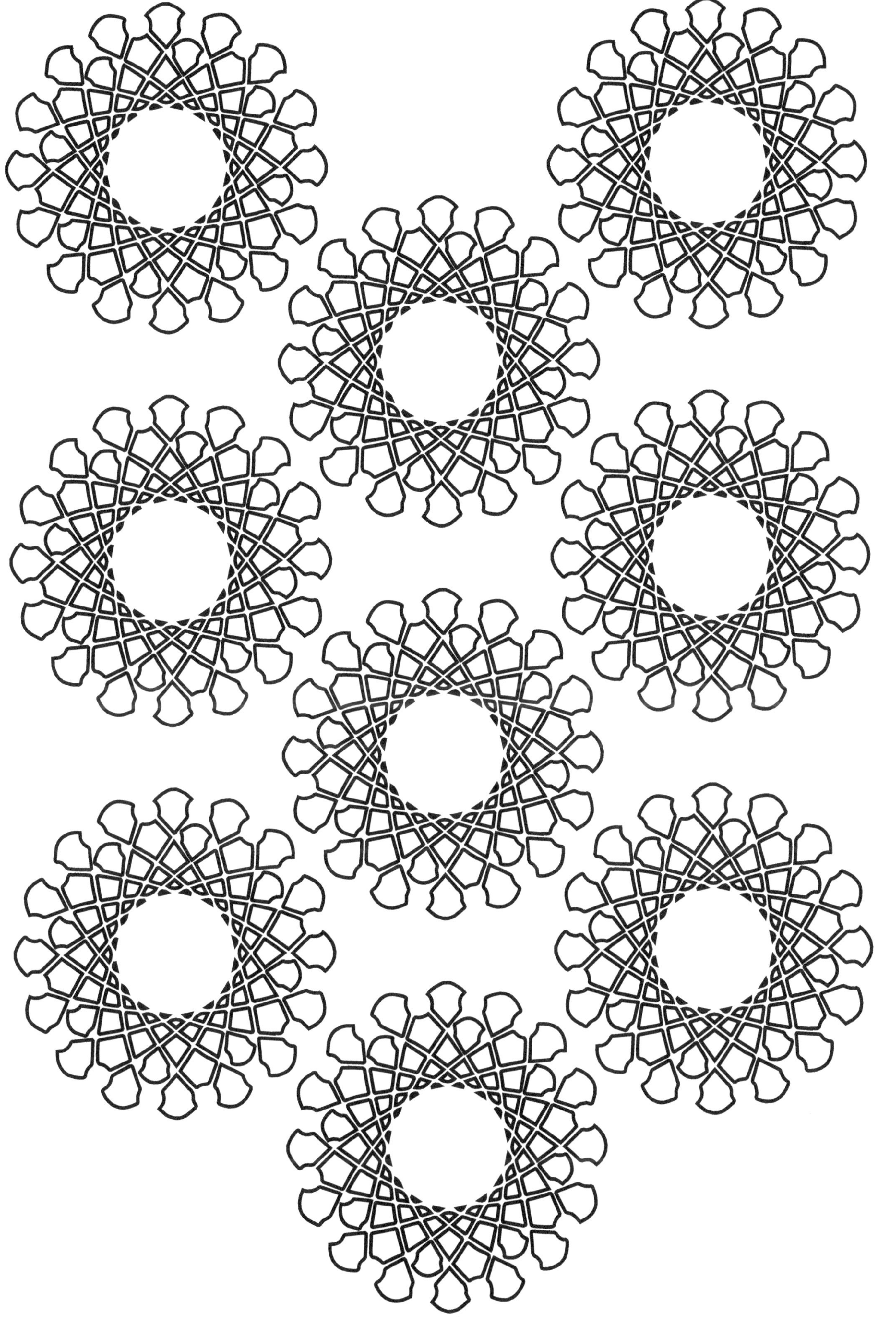

www.ingramcontent.com/pod-product-compliance
Lightning Source LLC
Chambersburg PA
CBHW081842250726
48659CB00008B/2562